SRA Prescriptive Spelling

A Basic Skills Program

A Division of The McGraw-Hill Companies

Columbus, Ohio

Credits

Formerly published by Barnell Loft, LTD. by William Wittenberg
Contributing Authors: Dr. Jean Wallace Gillet and Dr. Charles Temple

Cover Photo: Eclipse Studio

www.sra4kids.com

SRA/McGraw-Hill

A Division of The **McGraw·Hill** *Companies*

Send all inquiries to:
SRA/McGraw-Hill
8787 Orion Place
Columbus, OH 43240-4027

Printed in the United States of America.

ISBN 0-07-568966-9

2 3 4 5 6 7 8 9 QPD 06 05 04 03

Table of Contents

Spelling Strategies

There are many different ways to learn how to spell. A **spelling strategy** is a plan or clue that can make learning to spell easier. These strategies will appear in different lessons throughout this book. Take some time to learn how each one can help you spell better.

Sound Pattern Strategies

Learn to listen to the sounds in a word. Then spell each sound. *(sit)*

Think about how the word looks. Most words look wrong when they do not have the right spelling. *(can, not cen)*

Try switching consonant letters without changing the vowel. *(bat, hat, rat, flat, splat) / (mat, mad, map, mask)*

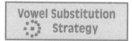

Try switching the vowel letters without changing the rest of the word. *(hit, hat, hut, hot) / (mane, mine) / (boat, beat)*

Think of a word that rhymes with the spelling word and has the same spelling pattern. *(cub, tub, rub)*

Structural Pattern Strategy

Think about the rules and exceptions you have learned for adding endings to words. *(crying, cried)*

Meaning Pattern Strategies

Think of how words from the same family are spelled. *(art, artist)*

Think about the meaning of the word to make sure you're using the right word. *(see, sea)*

Break the compound into its two words to spell each word. *(homework, home work)*

Think of foreign word spellings that are different from English spelling patterns. *(ballet)*

Check your writing carefully for spelling mistakes.

Find the word in a dictionary to make sure your spelling is correct.

Review Simple Consonant Sound Spellings

Many words are spelled the way they sound. Listen for the sound of the **consonant** at the beginning or ending of the words below. Notice how each consonant sounds like its letter name.

/b/ is spelled *b* as in *bad* and *bib* /n/ is spelled *n* as in *nest* and *man*

/d/ is spelled *d* as in *dash* and *mad* /p/ is spelled *p* as in *pin* and *jump*

/f/ is spelled *f* as in *fast* and *if* /r/ is spelled *r* as in *rug* and *fur*

/j/ is spelled *j* as in *jog* /s/ is spelled *s* as in *sand*

/k/ is spelled *k* as in *kiss* /t/ is spelled *t* as in *tip* and *sit*

/l/ is spelled *l* as in *lot* and *pool* /v/ is spelled *v* as in *vat*

/m/ is spelled *m* as in *map* and *trim* /z/ is spelled *z* as in *zip*

HINTS	EXAMPLES
Some consonants do not sound like their letter names.	
The /h/ sound does not sound like the letter *h*.	has
The /w/ sound does not sound like the letter *w*.	wish
The /y/ sound does not sound like the letter *y*.	yes

The letter *c* has hard and soft sounds.
  hard c: /k/ is spelled c
  soft c: /s/ is spelled c
	can
	cell

The letter *g* has hard and soft sounds.
  hard g: /g/ is spelled g
  soft g: /j/ is spelled g
	gum
	gym

The /ks/ sound as in *ax* or the /gz/ sound as in *exact* are spelled with the letter *x*.	
Exceptions	**Example**
In one word, the /f/ sound spelled *f* does not say its letter name at the end.	The f in *of* sounds like the /v/ sound.

Sound and Sort

Sorting words by their beginning and ending sounds can help you spell words with the same sounds.

 **Pronunciation Strategy**

Say each word in the box carefully. Write each word in the box below the word that has the same beginning consonant sound.

yesterday	battle	nylon	decide	pupil

boat   **d**inner   **n**ice

1. ___battle___   3. _____   5. _____

puppet   **y**ell

2. _____   4. _____

Say each word in the box carefully. Write each word in the box below the word that has the same ending consonant sound.

bear	rowboat	until	relief	blind

pi**ll**   fi**t**   i**f**

1. _____   3. _____   5. _____

bi**d**   oa**r**

2. _____   4. _____

Count 1 point for each correctly sorted word in both exercises.

_____ My Score
10 Top Score

Name _____

Listen and Link

Listening carefully for beginning and ending consonant sounds can help you spell words that have the same sounds.

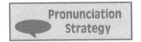
Pronunciation Strategy

To make a chain, link the last letter sound of the first word to the same first letter sound of another word. Continue until you have linked four words in each set. Write them in the blanks. Each chain is started for you.

Example: (band) — (deck) — (king) — (gift)

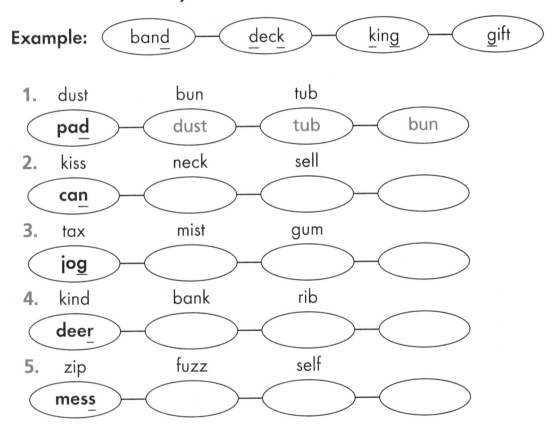

1. dust   bun   tub

    (**pad**) — (dust) — (tub) — (bun)

2. kiss   neck   sell

    (**can**) — (   ) — (   ) — (   )

3. tax   mist   gum

    (**jog**) — (   ) — (   ) — (   )

4. kind   bank   rib

    (**deer**) — (   ) — (   ) — (   )

5. zip   fuzz   self

    (**mess**) — (   ) — (   ) — (   )

Count 3 points for each correctly formed chain.   _____ My Score
                                                          15 Top Score

Review Sound Spellings • **3**

Sound and Sort

Listening for beginning consonant sounds can help you learn to spell words with those sounds.

Listen carefully to the beginning consonant sound of each word in the lists below. Choose a word from Lists 1, 2, 3, and 4 with the same consonant sound and write one word on each line to make a sentence.

List 1	List 2	List 3	List 4
Pretty	Harry	likes	peaches
Handsome	Suzie	finds	spoons
Funny	Leo	sells	hamburgers
Little	Polly	hates	feathers
Silly	Francis	picks	lollipops

Example: Beautiful   Betty   bakes   beans.

1. ____Pretty____   Polly   picks   peaches.

2. _____ _____ _____ _____

3. _____ _____ _____ _____

4. _____ _____ _____ _____

5. _____ _____ _____ _____

Count 1 point for each correctly chosen word in each sentence.

_____ My Score

20 Top Score

Lesson 2 — PROBLEM SOLVING

Short Vowel Letter Spellings

Vowels can make short or long sounds and have many different spellings. The position of the vowel in a word helps decide the vowel's sound. Most **short vowel sounds** have just one spelling.

Short Vowel Sounds

/a/ is spelled *a* as in *at* and *pal*   /o/ is spelled *o* as in *ox* and *hop*

/e/ is spelled *e* as in *elf* and *help*   /u/ is spelled *u* as in *up* and *jug*

/i/ is spelled *i* as in *it* and *fill*

HINTS	EXAMPLES
Every word has at least one vowel.	as, mess, bit, flop, up
Short vowels do not sound like their letters names.	The /a/ sound in *am* does not sound like the letter a.

Short vowel sounds most often are found in:
    words beginning with a vowel or
 	
    words with *vowel-consonant* endings
	u̲s, a̲t, e̲nd, i̲s, o̲x
	
	fa̱t, ste̱m, ri̱p, co̱t, nu̱t

Exceptions	**Examples**
The /u/ sound is spelled *o* in some words.	so̱n, to̱n
The letter *u* does not always say the /u/ sound. It can say the /o͞o/ sound as in *book*.	pu̱sh, pu̱ll

Sound and Sort

Say each word in the box carefully. Circle the words with the /a/ sound.

best	(dad)	lash	path	stuck
chop	fix	map	rest	tag

Count 2 points for each correctly circled word.   _____ My Score
                                              10 Top Score   Short Vowel Letter Spellings • **5**

Name _____

Rhyme Time

Knowing how to spell words ending with the same *vowel-consonant* sounds can help you spell other words that have the same endings.

 **Rhyming Strategy** **Sort words from the box by writing them below their rhyming *vowel-consonant* sound endings.**

cash	click	shop	stick	trump
chop	dump	spell	trash	well

-ash

1. _____cash_____

2. _____

-ell

5. _____

6. _____

-ump

9. _____

10. _____

-ick

3. _____

4. _____

-op

7. _____

8. _____

Sort words from the box by writing them below these common endings.

hill	slap	spill	trap	trot

-ill

1. _____

2. _____

-ap

3. _____

4. _____

-ot

5. _____

Count 1 point for each correctly sorted word.

_____ My Score

15 Top Score

Sort It Out

Sorting words with the same short vowel spellings can help you
spell other words with the same short vowel sounds.

 **Visualization Strategy** **Sort the words in the box by writing them under the correct heading.**

black	nest	snack	tip	vest
crest	slip	tack	track	west
drip	smack	test	trip	zip

Words with -ack

1. _____track_____

2. _____

3. _____

4. _____

5. _____

Words with -est

11. _____

12. _____

13. _____

14. _____

15. _____

Words with -ip

6. _____

7. _____

8. _____

9. _____

10. _____

Count 1 point for each
correctly sorted word.   _____ My Score
                                 15 Top Score

Short Vowel Letter Spellings • **7**

Rhyme Time

Listening for words with the same *vowel-consonant* sounds can help you learn to create poems that rhyme.

Example: It's lots of *fun*
to play in the *sun*.

 **Rhyming Strategy** **Choose words from the box that rhyme with the underlined word in each poem. Write each rhyming word in the blank to complete the rhyming sentence.**

bag	band	bump	camp	fish
flash	hen	lid	test	truck

1. Please put a <u>tag</u>
   on this brown ___bag___.

2. This is the <u>best</u>
   I've done on a _____.

3. I'll take out the <u>trash</u>
   and be back in a _____!

4. Do you have a <u>stamp</u>
   to mail a letter from _____?

5. What do you think I <u>did</u>
   with the jelly jar _____?

6. I saw ten <u>men</u>
   chase a red _____.

7. The car went <u>thump</u>
   when we went over the _____.

8. If you could make just one <u>wish</u>,
   would you choose to be a _____?

9. I don't think that <u>duck</u>
   wants to ride in a _____.

10. Isn't it just <u>grand</u>
    to see the marching _____?

Count 1 point for each correctly chosen rhyming word.

_____ My Score
10 Top Score

Long Vowel Letter Spellings

Long vowels sound like their letter names. Long vowel sounds have many different spelling patterns.

HINTS	EXAMPLES
When a word is a vowel or ends in a vowel, the vowel is usually long.	a, be, I, so
When a word has a *vowel-consonant-e* pattern, the vowel is long.	hate, these, rice, note, cute
The /ā/ sound can be spelled *a, a-consonant-e, ai,* and *ay.* The pattern *a* is usually found at the beginnings of words, and *ay* is found at the ends of words.	ate pain say
The /ē/ sound can be spelled *e, e-consonant-e, ee,* and *ea.* The patterns *ee* and *ea* are often found in the middles or ends of words.	here seen, see meal, sea
The /ī/ sound can be spelled *i, i-consonant-e, ie, igh, i* before *nd,* and *y* at the end of a word.	nice tie fight kind sky
The /ō/ sound can be spelled *o, o-consonant-e, oa,* and *ow.*	so role own, show boat, oak
The /yo͞o/ sound can be spelled *u* and *u-consonant-e.*	unit cube
The /o͞o/ sound can be spelled *u-consonant-e, oo, ew,* and *ue.*	tube cool new clue
Exceptions	
Long vowel sounds have many spelling exceptions. For example, a few words with the /ā/ sound spelled *ai* end in silent *e,* like *raise.*	

Pattern Pros

Knowing the long vowel sound spelling patterns can help you
learn to spell many new words.

 **Rhyming Strategy**   **Write the /ā/ sound patterns _a-consonant-e, ai,_ or _ay_ in the blanks to make a new word that rhymes with the given word. Then write the new words on the lines.**

1. tr<u>ai</u>l   n ___ai___ l   _____nail_____

2. s<u>ay</u>   h _____   _____

3. pr<u>ai</u>se   r _____ se   _____

4. h<u>ai</u>l   j _____ l   _____

5. h<u>ate</u>   d _____ t _____   _____

 **Rhyming Strategy**   **Write the /ē/ sound patterns _e, e-consonant-e, ee,_ or _ea_ in the blanks to make a new word that rhymes with the given word. Then write the new words on the lines.**

6. dr<u>ea</u>m   t _____ m   _____

7. k<u>ee</u>p   w _____ p   _____

8. b<u>e</u>   m _____   _____

9. m<u>ea</u>l   s _____ l   _____

10. gr<u>ee</u>n   s _____ n   _____

Count 1 point for each
correctly spelled word.   _____ My Score

                 10 Top Score

Sensible Sort

Sorting words by the same long vowel patterns will help you
spell words with the same patterns.

 **Family Strategy** **Sort the words in the boxes by writing them below the words with the same /ī/, /ō/, or /o͞o/ sound patterns.**

dry	grind	light	might	try

bright   **cry**   **hind**

1. _____light_____   3. _____   5. _____

2. _____   4. _____

blow	row	soap	toast	tote

snow   **boat**   **note**

1. _____   3. _____   5. _____

2. _____   4. _____

flew	glue	school	stew	true

new   **clue**   **pool**

1. _____   3. _____   5. _____

2. _____   4. _____

Count 1 point for each
correctly sorted word.   _____ My Score
                                    15 Top Score   Long Vowel Letter Spellings • 11

Look Sharp

Thinking about spelling patterns and how a word looks can help you spell words with long vowel sounds.

 **Visualization Strategy**

Look carefully at the two spellings for each word. Think about how the word should look. Circle the correct spelling for each word. Write the correct spelling on the line.

1. (grape)   greap   _____grape_____

2. tun   tune   _____

3. trale   trail   _____

4. tra   tray   _____

5. keap   keep   _____

6. myght   might   _____

7. sky   skay   _____

8. blow   blo   _____

9. flew   floo   _____

10. mune   moon   _____

11. roast   rost   _____

12. blinde   blind   _____

13. thi   thigh   _____

14. snow   sno   _____

15. mean   meen   _____

Count 1 point for each correctly spelled word.

_____ My Score

15 Top Score

Name _____

Review Sound Spellings

These exercises review what you have learned in Lessons 1–3.
Refer to those lessons if you have difficulty completing an
exercise.

Lesson 1 Review Simple Consonant Sound Spellings

 **Pronunciation Strategy**   **Sort each word in the box under the word that has the same beginning consonant sound.**

voice	dirty	second	market	very
borrow	dozen	sister	manners	beneath

b__ad

1. ___beneath___

2. _____

d__ash

5. _____

6. _____

m__ap

9. _____

10. _____

s__and

3. _____

4. _____

v__at

7. _____

8. _____

Lesson 2 Short Vowel Letter Spellings

Rhyming Strategy   **Sort the words in the box by writing them next to their short vowel endings.**

junk	link	spank	thank	think

-ank

1. ___thank___

2. _____

-ink

3. _____

4. _____

-unk

5. _____

Count 1 point for each
correctly sorted word in
both exercises.

_____ My Score
15 Top Score

Name _____

Lesson 3 Long Vowel Letter Spellings

 **Visualization Strategy**

Choose which long vowel sound spelling is correct. Circle the correct spelling in each pair. Write the correct spelling on the line.

1. ray   rai   _____
2. ait   ate   _____
3. gowt   goat   _____
4. try   tri   _____
5. clew   clue   _____

6. leight light _____
7. find   finde _____
8. thro   throw _____
9. smile   smil   _____
10. knea   knee   _____

Cumulative Review

 **Proofreading Strategy**

Read the following sentences. Five misspelled words can be found within the text. Cross out each misspelled word and write the correct spelling above the word.

When Helen Keller was a baby, an illness left her deaf and ~~blynd~~ *blind*. She would

scream and cri when she became angry and upset. Helen's parents found a

teecher for her. Her naim was Anne Sullivan. Anne taught Helen how to read

and speek.

Count 1 point for each
correctly spelled word.   _____ My Score
                                   15 Top Score

Vowel Spellings (ou, ow, oi, oy)

Four main spelling patterns exist for words that have the **/ou/** and **/oi/** sounds: **ou, ow, oi, oy.** Notice how the two letters together make only one sound.

HINTS	EXAMPLES

The /ou/ sound is usually spelled ow:
    in the middle of a word when *l, n,* or *d* is the last letter
    or at the end of words
	fowl, town, cr<u>ow</u>d
	 h<u>ow</u>, c<u>ow</u>

The /ou/ sound is often spelled ou:
    at the beginning of a word
    or in the middle of a word not ending in *l, n,* or *d*
	<u>ou</u>ch
	 cr<u>ou</u>ch, h<u>ou</u>nd

The /oi/ sound is spelled *oi* at the beginning and in the middle of words.	<u>oi</u>l b<u>oi</u>l
The /oi/ sound is spelled *oy* at the end of a word and sometimes at the end of a syllable.	b<u>oy</u> l<u>oy</u>-al
Twice as many words spell the /ou/ sound with ou than with ow.	c<u>ou</u>ch cl<u>ow</u>n
When you hear the /ou/ sound at the end of a word, spell it ow.	n<u>ow</u>
When you hear the /oi/ sound at the end of a word, spell it oy.	j<u>oy</u>
Exceptions	**Examples**
A few words spell the /oi/ sound with oy at the beginning of a word.	<u>oy</u>ster
One word spells the /ou/ sound with ou at the end.	th<u>ou</u>
Sometimes ow also can sound like the /ō/ sound.	gl<u>ow</u>

Sound and Sort

Sorting words by the /ou/ and /oi/ sounds can help you spell words with the same sound.

 **Say each word in the box carefully. Listen for the position of the /ou/ sound in each word. Write each word in the box under the word that has the /ou/ sound in the same position in the word.**

frown	out	plow	south	vow

cow   **town**   **owl**

1. ____vow____   3. _____   5. _____

2. _____   4. _____

Simple Sort

 **Say each word in the box carefully. Listen for the position of the /oi/ sound in each word. Write each word in the box under the word that has the /oi/ sound in the same position in the word.**

cowboy	enjoy	joint	oyster	voice

boy   **boil**   **oil**

1. ____enjoy____   3. _____   5. _____

2. _____   4. _____

Count 1 point for each correctly sorted word.

_____ My Score
10 Top Score

Look Smart

Looking for the position of the /ou/ and /oi/ sounds in words can help you learn how to spell words with those sounds.

 **Visualization Strategy** **Look carefully at each pair of words. Circle the word with the correct /ou/ sound spelling. Write the correct spelling on the line.**

1. (allow)   allou   <u>allow</u>

2. nown   noun   _____

3. slouch   slowch   _____

4. clown   cloun   _____

5. rownd   round   _____

Look Sharp

 **Visualization Strategy** **Look carefully at each pair of words. Circle the word with the correct /oi/ sound spelling. Write the correct spelling on the line.**

1. poynt   (point)   <u>point</u>

2. destroy   destroi   _____

3. noise   noyse   _____

4. cowboi   cowboy   _____

5. choice   choyce   _____

Listen As You Learn

Listening for the /ou/ and /oi/ sounds can help you learn to spell words with those sound spelling patterns.

Pronunciation Strategy

Read each sentence carefully. Listen for words with the /ou/ and /oi/ sounds. Circle and then write all the words with those sounds in the blanks. Can you find all 30 words?

1. (Roy) is a rodeo (cowboy.) Roy _____ cowboy _____

2. He mounts an angry bull and coils the rope around his hand. _____
   _____

3. At the sound of a buzzer, Roy and the bull spring out of the chute. _____
   _____ _____

4. The bull turns round and round, trying to throw Roy to the ground. _____
   _____ _____ _____

5. The noisy crowd howls to cheer on the cowboy. _____ _____
   _____ _____

6. The rodeo clowns wait to distract the bull if he bucks the rider off. _____

7. The buzzer sounds, and the cowboy quickly dismounts. _____
   _____ _____

8. The crowd applauds Roy loudly, and the other cowhands join in. _____
   _____ _____ _____ _____

9. Roy is overjoyed. _____ _____

10. He is proud to be crowned "Cowboy of the Year." _____ _____
    _____

Count 1 point for each correctly chosen word.

_____ My Score
30 Top Score

Lesson 5 | PROBLEM SOLVING

r-controlled Vowel Spellings

When the letter **r** follows a vowel, the sound of the vowel is changed by the r and is pronounced as one sound. These new sounds, /**âr**/, /**ûr**/, and /**ôr**/, are called **r-controlled vowel sounds.**

HINTS	EXAMPLES	
The /**âr**/ sound can be spelled: are as in *share* air as in *chair*	r<u>are</u>	h<u>air</u>
The /**âr**/ sound can be spelled: ar as in *car*	art farm	

The /**ûr**/ sound can be spelled:
   ear as in *earn*   ir as in *bird*
   or as in *worm*   ur as in *burn*
   er as in *her*
	p<u>ear</u>l
	w<u>or</u>d
	cl<u>er</u>k
		ch<u>ir</u>p
		n<u>ur</u>se

The /**ôr**/ sound can be spelled:
   ore as in *core*   or as in *for*
                oar as in *roar*
	sn<u>ore</u>	b<u>or</u>n
		b<u>oar</u>d

Most *r*-controlled vowel sound spellings are found in words with just one syllable.	word, purse	
Exceptions	**Examples**	
The /**ûr**/ sound + e has the /ī/ sound as in *fire*.	tire	
The /**ûr**/ sound + e has the /y$\overline{oo}$/ sound as in *cure*.	pure	
The /**âr**/ sound is spelled *ere* as in *there*.	where, here	
The /**ôr**/ sound is spelled *oor* as in *floor*.	door	
The /**ôr**/ sound is spelled *ar* as in *warn*.	ward	

Sort It Out

Sorting words by their *r*-controlled vowel sounds can help you spell words with the same vowel sounds.

 Visualization Strategy

Listen carefully to the *r*-controlled vowel sound in each word. Sort the words in the box under the correct heading.

fair	mare	pear	square	stair

Words with *-air*

1. _____ stair _____

2. _____

Words with *-are*

3. _____

4. _____

Words with *-ear*

5. _____

Listen and Look

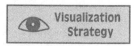 Visualization Strategy

Listen carefully to the *r*-controlled vowel sound in each word. Sort the words in the box under the correct heading.

board	chore	cork	short	swore

Words with *-or*

1. _____ cork _____

2. _____

Words with *-ore*

3. _____

4. _____

Words with *-oar*

5. _____

Count 1 point for each correctly sorted word.

_____ My Score

10 Top Score

Spell Check

Looking for the correct spellings of words can help you learn to spell words with the /ûr/, /ôr/, and /âr/ sounds.

 **Visualization Strategy** | **Each pair of words can be pronounced the same, but only one is spelled correctly. Circle the word that spells the /ûr/ sound correctly and write it on the line.**

1. furst (first)   _first_   4. worm   werm   _____

2. bird   burd   _____   5. pearse   purse   _____

3. girm   germ   _____

 **Visualization Strategy** | **Circle the word that spells the /ôr/ sound correctly. Write the correct spelling on the line.**

1. roar   rore   _____   4. form   foarm   _____

2. boarn   born   _____   5. fore   foar   _____

3. mor   more   _____

 **Visualization Strategy** | **Circle the word that spells the /âr/ sound correctly. Write the correct spelling on the line.**

1. (bear)   bair   _____   4. scare   scair   _____

2. har   hair   _____   5. wair   wear   _____

3. chear   chair   _____

Powerful Proofreading

Proofreading is a tool used by good spellers that can help you learn the correct spelling of words.

Visualization Strategy

Look at each sentence carefully. Circle the word in parentheses that has the correctly spelled *r*-controlled vowel sound. Write the word on the line.

1. Weather forecasters can predict where (storms, stoarms) will occur.

   _____

2. Some (yeers, years) forecasters track more than 20 hurricanes.

   _____

3. A center of low pressure (forems, forms) in the Atlantic Ocean.

   _____

4. Winds begin to (whirl, wherl) around it.

   _____

5. A weather satellite passing over the area shows what forecasters (feer, fear).

   _____

6. A hurricane is (born, boarn).

   _____

7. Hurricanes that affect the East Coast of the United States usually travel (noarth, north).

   _____

8. Fortunately, they sometimes (curve, cirve) away and miss the land.

   _____

9. Parts of Florida often receive the (wurst, worst) of the violent weather.

   _____

10. Winds of 100 miles per hour (tair, tear) off roofs from homes and businesses.

    _____

Count 1 point for each correctly chosen word.

_____ My Score
10 Top Score

Final Consonant Blends (mp, nd, nk, nt)

Final consonant blends are groups of consonants at the end of a word in which each letter is heard, like the /mp/ sound of the mp in the word *jump*. The final consonant blends **mp, nd, nk,** and **nt** are found at the end of one-syllable words.

/mp/ is spelled mp as in *ca<u>mp</u>*   /nk/ is spelled nk as in *ba<u>nk</u>*

/nd/ is spelled nd as in *sa<u>nd</u>*   /nt/ is spelled nt as in *a<u>nt</u>*

HINTS	EXAMPLES
The final consonant blends *mp, nd, nk,* and *nt* are not found at the beginning of words. Most often, the vowel that comes before the consonant blend has a short vowel sound.	lamp, pond, trunk, spent
The /ou/ sound sometimes comes before *nd*.	f<u>ou</u>nd, gr<u>ou</u>nd
Many *mp, nd, nk,* and *nt* words have rhyming patterns.	lump/pump, end/bend, tank/sank, bent/went
Exceptions	**Examples**
The /nt/ sound rarely occurs after a long vowel.	pint

Sound and Sort

Circle the ending consonant blends in the words below.

bra(nd)	dent	hand	sank	scent

Lesson 6

Listen and Learn

Listening for the final consonant blends in words can help you
learn how to spell other words with the same ending patterns.

 **Visualization Strategy** | **Look for the final consonant blend in each word in the box. Sort the words in the box under the correct headings.**

| brand | damp | grand | ramp | tramp |

Words That End Like *camp*

1. _____damp_____

2. _____

3. _____

Word That End Like *sand*

4. _____

5. _____

| plank | rent | sent | shrank | spent |

Words That End Like *cent*

6. _____

7. _____

8. _____

Word That End Like *bank*

9. _____

10. _____

Count 1 point for each _____ My Score
correctly sorted word.   10 Top Score

Reason to Rhyme

Sorting words by their rhyming patterns can help you spell other words with the same spelling patterns.

 **Rhyming Strategy**

Listen carefully to the vowels preceding the /nt/ sound in each word in the box. Sort the words below the correct headings.

hunt	plant	scent	slant	spent

Words That Rhyme with *ant*	**Words That Rhyme with *rent***	**Words That Rhyme with *runt***
1. _____plant_____	3. _____	5. _____
2. _____	4. _____	

Adding Ending Sounds

 **Dictionary Strategy**

Add the final consonant blends *nk*, *mp*, or *nt* to the letters that will spell real words. If you are unsure whether the word is a real word, check your spelling in the dictionary.

ha___   **sa___**   **ra___**

1. _____hank_____   2. _____   3. _____

                                                         4. _____

                                                         5. _____

Count 1 point for each correctly sorted word in the first exercise. Count 1 point for each correctly spelled word in the second exercise.

_____ My Score
10 Top Score

Final Consonant Blends • **25**

Spell Check

Looking for words with correct spellings can help you learn how
to spell words with consonant blends.

 **Visualization Strategy**

**Think how words look with the final consonant
blends *mp*, *nd*, *nk*, and *nt*. Circle the word in each
pair that has the correct spelling to make a real
word. Write the correct spelling on the line.**

1.	yand	(yank)	yank
2.	dunt	dump	_____
3.	cramp	crand	_____
4.	thint	think	_____
5.	count	coung	_____
6.	bunt	bund	_____
7.	thank	thang	_____
8.	samp	sand	_____
9.	vent	veng	_____
10.	found	foump	_____

Count 1 point for each
correctly chosen word.

_____ My Score

10 Top Score

Name _____

Review *Sound Spelling Patterns*

These exercises will review what you have learned in Lessons 4–6.
Refer to those lessons if you have difficulty completing an exercise.

Lesson 4 *Vowel Spellings (ou, ow, oi, oy)*

Sort each word in the box under the word that has the same /ou/ or /oi/ sound in the same position.

| ahoy | outboard | plow | power | toilet |

how   **out**   **soil**

1. _____ 3. _____ 5. _____

south   **toy**

2. _____ 4. _____

Lesson 5 *r-controlled Vowel Spellings*

Sort each word in the box by writing it under the word with the same *r*-controlled vowel sound, not necessarily the same *r*-controlled vowel spelling.

| circle | farmhouse | garbage | person | storehouse |

carpet   **perfect**   **forty**

1. _____ 3. _____ 5. _____

2. _____ 4. _____

Count 1 point for each   _____ My Score
correctly sorted word in
both exercises.   10 Top Score

Name _____

Lesson 6 *Final Consonant Blends (mp, nd, nk, nt)*

Listen carefully to the *nd* and *nt* final consonant sounds of the words in the box. Sort the two-syllable words in the box by writing them under the words with the same final consonant blend.

amount	basement	husband	moment	pretend
background	beyond	legend	patent	urgent

hand   **plant**

1. _____   4. _____   6. _____   9. _____

2. _____   5. _____   7. _____   10. _____

3. _____   8. _____

Cumulative Review

Read the following sentences. Cross out the ten misspelled words and write the correct spellings above the words.

brink

In 1999, the eastern United States was on the ~~brinc~~ of disaster. There wus a

drought, and the farmers were feerful that they would not have a hervast to plou.

The rain shours finally came in large amownts, causing a flud. The government had

to respong during this ergant time of need.

Count 1 point for each correctly sorted word _____ My Score
in the first exercise. Count 1 point for each   20 Top Score
correctly spelled word in the second exercise.

Consonant Blends (s-blends)

Remember, **consonant blends** are groups of two or three consonants in which each letter is pronounced. Many consonant blends can be found at the beginning or end of a word. This lesson focuses on the **s-blends,** blends that start with the letter **s,** as well as some more blends found only at the ends of words.

Two-letter s-blends:

/sl/   is spelled sl as in slip   /sm/   is spelled sm as in smell

/sp/   is spelled sp as in speak   /sn/   is spelled sn as in snow

/sk/   is spelled sk as in sky   /st/   is spelled st as in stack

/sk/   is spelled sc as in scare   /sw/   is spelled sw as in swim

Three-letter s-blends:

/skr/   is spelled scr as in scream   /spr/   is spelled spr as in spray

/spl/   is spelled spl as in split   /str/   is spelled str as in string

More blends found at the ends of words:

/ft/   is spelled ft as in gift   /lk/   is spelled lk as in milk

/ld/   is spelled ld as in bald   /lp/   is spelled lp as in help

/lf/   is spelled lf as in elf   /lt/   is spelled lt as in wilt

HINTS	EXAMPLES
The blends sc and sk spell the /sk/ sound.	scold, skin
When you hear the /sk/ sound at the end of a word, spell it sk, not sc.	ask
Only a few words end with sp.	wasp, lisp
Exceptions	
The sc in science makes the /s/ sound, not the /sk/ sound.	
The /sk/ sound is spelled sch as in school and scheme.	
The l is not heard in half and calf.	

Sound and Sort

Sorting words by beginning s-blends can help you spell other words with the same beginning sounds.

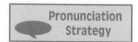
Pronunciation Strategy

Listen carefully to the sound the two or three letters make at the beginning of each word in the box. Sort the words in the box under the word with the same underlined sound.

---

splatter	slick	sprain	swat	strangle	swarm	scrimp	smash	sprinkle
stretch	sleet	scramble	smug	splendid	sweep	spruce	stroke	
scratch	sweat	splash	smile	sprout	slide	screech	splinter	

---

scream

1. scramble
2. _____
3. _____
4. _____

split

5. _____
6. _____
7. _____
8. _____

spray

9. _____
10. _____
11. _____
12. _____

string

13. _____
14. _____
15. _____

slip

16. _____
17. _____
18. _____

smell

19. _____
20. _____
21. _____

swim

22. _____
23. _____
24. _____
25. _____

Count 1 point for each correctly sorted word.

_____ My Score

25 Top Score

Rhyming Words

Removing one letter from some words with consonant blends
can help you spell other words with consonant blends.

 **Rhyming Strategy** **Remove the letter shown from each three-letter consonant blend to make a new rhyming word with a two-letter blend. Write the new word on the line.**

Three-Letter Blends **Two-Letter Blends**

1. splash – *p* = ___slash___

2. string – *r* = _____

3. split – *l* = _____

4. split – *p* = _____

5. splat – *p* = _____

Sound Sort

Listening for beginning and ending consonant blends can help
you learn how to spell words with the same consonant blends.

 **Pronunciation Strategy** **Listen to the sound made by each underlined ending consonant blend. Choose a word from the box that begins with the same consonant blend as the underlined blend and write it on the line.**

| sky | spin | stem | step | stomp |

1. be<u>st</u> ___stem___

2. ta<u>sk</u> _____

3. wa<u>sp</u> _____

4. che<u>st</u> _____

5. cru<u>st</u> _____

Proofreading Power

Proofreading can help you learn to notice and correct spelling errors.

 **Visualization Strategy**

Read each sentence carefully. Look at the words in parentheses. Circle the word with the correct consonant blend spelling and write it on the line.

1. Primitive people lived in caves and treetops to protect themselves from (wild, wilt) beasts. _____wild_____

2. When people began to use tools, they built (stonger, stronger) places to live. _____

3. Castles were made of (stone, splone) _____.

4. When machines were invented, the (tast, task) of keeping people safe became important. _____

5. Operating machines safely became a concern, and (skores, scores) of laws were passed to protect workers. _____

6. After cars were invented, roads and highways were (builf, built) _____.

7. People were put at (risk, risp) because cars could travel quickly on the highways. _____

8. Driving at high (spreeds, speeds) causes many accidents. _____

9. (Special, Splecial) safety devices in automobiles, such as seat belts and air bags, can prevent many injuries. _____

10. Safety education can (help, helf) make people aware of ways they can protect themselves and others from accidents. _____

Count 1 point for each correctly chosen word.

_____ My Score
10 Top Score

Lesson 8   PROBLEM SOLVING

Consonant Digraphs

Remember, the sound of each letter in a **consonant blend** is heard. However, in a **consonant digraph,** the two or three letters make a single new sound.

/ch/	is spelled *ch* as in *child* and *much*	*choke, teach*
/ch/	is spelled *tch* as in *watch*	*match*
/kw/	is spelled *qu* as in *quilt*	*quick*
/sh/	is spelled *sh* as in *shine* and *wish*	*shore, push, shush*
/th/	is spelled *th* as *think* and *breathe*	*thumb, bathe*
/wh/	is spelled *wh* as in *what*	*where*

HINTS	EXAMPLES
The digraphs *qu* and *wh* are not used at the ends of words.	quiet, when
Some digraphs are joined with another consonant letter to form a consonant blend as in:	th + r three sh + r shriek
Exceptions	**Examples**
The /sh/ sound is spelled *s* as in *sure*.	sugar
The /sh/ sound is spelled *ch* as in *chute*.	machine
The /h/ sound is spelled *wh* as in *who*.	whole
The /k/ sound is spelled *ch* as in *stomach*.	choral, orchestra, orchid

Short Sort

 **Visualization Strategy**   **Circle the consonant digraph in each word.**

wa(sh)	tooth	choke	quit	shall

Count 2 points for each   _____ My Score
correctly circled digraph.   10 Top Score

Sound and Sort

Noticing digraph sounds can help you become a better speller.

 **Pronunciation Strategy** **Listen carefully to the consonant digraph sound in each word. Sort the words in the box by writing them under the correct headings.**

brush	beach	chant	rich	dish
shallow	charge	thunder	much	shell
thankful	shoe	chap	mash	thief
chest	fresh	bunch	thimble	ship

Words That End Like teach

1. ____much____
2. _____
3. _____
4. _____

Words That End Like wish

5. _____
6. _____
7. _____
8. _____

Words That Begin Like thick

9. _____
10. _____
11. _____
12. _____

Words That Begin Like share

13. _____
14. _____
15. _____
16. _____

Words That Begin Like child

17. _____
18. _____
19. _____
20. _____

Count 1 point for each correctly sorted word.

_____ My Score
20 Top Score

Rhyme Time

Listening carefully to the vowel sound and the final digraph
sound can help you learn how to spell rhyming words.

 **Rhyming Strategy** | **Sort the words from the box below the rhyming word.**

| blush | crash | lunch | munch | squish |
| brush | fish | math | path | trash |

brunch   **mash**   **wish**   **rush**   **bath**

1. munch   3. _____   5. _____   7. _____   9. _____

2. _____   4. _____   6. _____   8. _____   10. _____

Digraph Sort

Sorting words by the consonant digraph sounds can help you
spell words with the same sounds.

 **Pronunciation Strategy** | **Listen carefully to the underlined consonant digraph sound in each word. Sort the words in the box under the word with the same digraph sound.**

| pathway | quietly | sherbet | teacher | whistle |

purch**ase**   **qu**ickly   **peri**sh   **th**ankful   **wh**imper

1. teacher   2. _____   3. _____   4. _____   5. _____

Count 1 point for each
correctly sorted word in
both exercises.

_____ My Score
15 Top Score

Consonant Digraphs • **35**

Chain Links

Listening carefully to consonant digraph sounds can help you choose words with the same sounds.

Pronunciation Strategy **Link the three words in parentheses to the first word so that each ending digraph or letter is linked to a word with the same digraph or letter at the beginning.**

Example: ma<u>ch</u> + <u>ch</u>il<u>d</u> + <u>d</u>as<u>h</u> + <u>sh</u>ip

1. tooth + _____their_____ + _____rush_____ + _____shame_____ (shame, rush, their)

2. peach + _____ + _____ + _____ (north, chin, thumb)

3. fresh + _____ + _____ + _____ (chicken, shall, lunch)

4. birth + _____ + _____ + _____ (chum, thanks, such)

Proofreading Power

Proofreading can help you learn how to look for the correct spelling of words with digraphs.

Visualization Strategy **Read each sentence carefully. Circle the word in parentheses with the correct spelling. Write the correct spelling on the line.**

1. Cardinals are one of the most popular songbirds in (Northe, (North)) America.
   _____North_____

2. The cardinal makes a (cheerful, sheerful) sound. _____

3. Cardinals often build their nests in brambly (buthes, bushes).

   _____

Count 1 point for each correctly chosen word in both exercises.

_____ My Score
15 Top Score

Lesson 9 PROBLEM SOLVING

Final /s/, /j/, /k/

Learning sound spelling patterns can help you spell words with
the ending **/s/**, **/j/**, and **/k/** sounds.

HINTS	EXAMPLES
The /s/ sound is often spelled *ss* after a short vowel sound.	pass, hiss
The /s/ sound is often spelled *c* with a *vowel-consonant-e* pattern.	slice, nice
The /j/ sound is spelled *ge* with a *vowel-consonant-e* pattern or when it follows an *r*-controlled vowel.	huge urge
The /j/ sound is spelled *dge* when it is preceded by a short vowel sound.	ledge
The /k/ sound is spelled *k* with a *vowel-consonant-e* pattern, when it follows a long vowel sound, or when it follows an *r*-controlled vowel.	hike, peek, fork
The /k/ sound is spelled *ck* when it follows a short vowel sound.	stuck, stick
Exceptions	**Examples**
The /s/ sound is not always spelled *ss* after a short vowel sound.	yes, bus, plus, us, gas, this
In a few words with the *vowel-consonant-e* pattern, the ending /s/ sound is spelled with the letter *s*, not the letter *c*.	erase, moose, loose
The /j/ sound is spelled *ge* when the short vowel sound is followed by *n*.	sponge, cringe
Sometimes the vowel before *nge* is long.	change
The /s/ sound is spelled *ce* after a short vowel sound followed by *n*.	dance

Look and Listen

Looking at a word carefully can help you see a pattern in its spelling.

 **Visualization Strategy** **Sort each word in the boxes with the final /j/, /k/, and /s/ sounds below the word with the same spelling pattern.**

edge	fudge	huge	large	stage

judge   **page**   **urge**

1. _____fudge_____   3. _____   5. _____

2. _____   4. _____

clerk	lick	rock	snake	week

cake   **speak**   **park**   **pack**

1. _____   2. _____   3. _____   4. _____

                                                      5. _____

class	kiss	mess	spice	trace

fuss   **place**

1. _____   4. _____

2. _____   5. _____

3. _____

Count 1 point for each correctly sorted word in all three exercises.

_____ My Score
15 Top Score

Word Building by Subtracting

Subtracting letters from some words can help you learn how to spell new rhyming words.

 **Rhyming Strategy** **Take out the letters shown from the words below to spell rhyming words. Write the new word on the line.**

1. trace   – tr   = ___ace___
2. twice   – tw   = _____
3. splurge – spl = _____
4. track   – t   = _____
5. stake   – s   = _____
6. stage   – st   = _____
7. trace   – t   = _____
8. flake   – f   = _____
9. pounce   – p   = _____
10. spark   – s   = _____

11. ledge   – l   = _____
12. crack   – c   = _____
13. stick   – s   = _____
14. class   – c   = _____
15. bridge   – b   = _____
16. spoke   – s   = _____
17. lace   – l   = _____
18. croak   – cr   = _____
19. shook   – s   = _____
20. pluck   – p   = _____

The Right Look

Thinking about how a word looks can help you spell it.

 **Visualization Strategy** | **Look carefully at the two spellings for each word. Circle the word with the correct /s/ sound spelling pattern. Write the correct spelling on the line.**

1. mece (mess) _____mess_____   4. class clace _____

2. slice sliss _____   5. twiss twice _____

3. trass trace _____

Circle the word with the correct /j/ sound spelling pattern. Write the correct spelling on the line.

1. large lardge _____   4. fudge fuge _____

2. dodge doge _____   5. plege pledge _____

3. stadge stage _____

Circle the word with the correct /k/ sound spelling pattern. Write the correct spelling on the line.

1. parke park _____   4. strike strik _____

2. peek peeck _____   5. quick quik _____

3. lake lak _____

Count 1 point for each correctly chosen word in all three exercises.

_____ My Score

15 Top Score

Name _____

Review Sound Spelling Patterns

These exercises review what you have learned in Lessons 7-9. Refer to those lessons if you have difficulty completing an exercise.

Lesson 7 Consonant Blends

Sort the words in the box by writing them next to the word with the same consonant blend.

smear	field	straw	slide	snail
crisp	risk	test	yelp	swat

1. slip _____
2. speak _____
3. ask _____
4. smell _____
5. snow _____

6. last _____
7. swim _____
8. string _____
9. bald _____
10. help _____

Lesson 8 Consonant Digraphs

Circle the consonant digraph in each word. Write the word on the line.

1. whine _____
2. wash _____
3. peach _____
4. shine _____
5. their _____

6. though _____
7. charge _____
8. shelf _____
9. quite _____
10. fresh _____

Count 1 point for each correctly sorted word in the first exercise. Count 1 point for each correctly circled digraph in the second exercise.

_____ My Score

20 Top Score

Name _____

Lesson 9 Final /s/, /j/, /k/

 **Rhyming Strategy** **Choose a word from the box that rhymes with one of the words below. Write the word next to its rhyming word.**

cake	clerk	hike	muss	stage
cheek	fork	ledge	place	truck
class	fudge	miss	stack	twice

1. pass _____
2. judge _____
3. trace _____
4. peek _____
5. kiss _____

6. stork _____
7. perk _____
8. pledge _____
9. mice _____
10. strike _____

11. flake _____
12. pack _____
13. fuss _____
14. page _____
15. stuck _____

Cumulative Review

Proofreading Strategy **Read the following sentences. Cross out the ten misspelled words. Write the correct spellings above the misspelled words.**

lived
Dinosaurs ~~lifed~~ on Urth many yeares ago. The dinosaur called the ankylosaur hed

bony playts down its syde. It used a nob on the ind of its tail like a klub. The

ankylosaur would swing its tail to defend itself from enemyes.

Count 1 point for each correctly chosen word in the first exercise. Count 1 point for each correctly spelled word in the second exercise.

_____ My Score
25 Top Score

42   **UNIT 3** Review: *Sound Spelling Patterns*

Adding -s and -es

A **singular noun,** like the word *dog*, means one person, place, idea, or thing. A **plural noun,** like *dogs*, is more than one person, place, idea, or thing.

HINTS	EXAMPLES
Add **-s** to most nouns to form the plural.	cat + s = cats
Add **-es** to nouns that end in *s, ss, sh, ch, x,* or *z* to make the noun plural.	gas + es = gases bosses, wishes, lunches, axes, buzzes
If a noun ends with *f* or *fe*, change the *f* or *fe* to *v*, and add **-es**.	half + es = halves wife + es = wives
Adding **-s** to a noun usually does not change the number of syllables in the word.	*map* has one syllable *maps* has one syllable
When **-es** is added to a noun, it usually adds another syllable to the word.	*gas* has one syllable *gases* has two syllables
Exceptions	**Examples**
When **-s** is added to some nouns ending in silent *e*, it adds another syllable to the word.	*horse* has one syllable *horses* has two syllables
Some nouns change their spellings when made plural.	man/men, ox/oxen, child/children
Some plural nouns have the same spelling as the singular noun.	one *sheep*, many *sheep*
Only a few nouns do not change *f* to *v* to form a plural.	one *serf*, several *serfs* one *whiff*, two *whiffs*

Making Nouns Plural

Adding plural endings to words can help you learn to spell the plural forms of other words.

Decide whether to add -s or -es to make each noun plural. Circle the correct plural ending. Write the plural form of the noun on the line.

Singular Nouns	Plural Endings		Plural Nouns
1. time	(-s)	-es	times
2. boy	-s	-es	
3. wish	-s	-es	
4. skirt	-s	-es	
5. nurse	-s	-es	
6. crutch	-s	-es	
7. box	-s	-es	
8. brook	-s	-es	
9. buzz	-s	-es	
10. match	-s	-es	

Change the f or fe to v in each word and add -es. Write the plural form on the line.

1. shelf _____shelves_____   4. wife _____

2. knife _____   5. elf _____

3. scarf _____

Count 1 point for each correctly spelled word in both exercises.   _____ My Score

15 Top Score

Plural Spelling Sounds

Listening to the number of syllables in a word can help you
learn how to spell the plural form of that word.

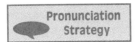

**Say each plural noun in the box. If the noun has one
syllable, the plural was made by adding -s. If the
noun has two syllables, the plural was made by
adding -es. Sort each plural noun in the box under
the correct heading.**

beaches	crashes	grapes	ranches	sketches
bikes	flames	hunches	rates	stones
bushes	flushes	notes	sales	strokes
buzzes	foxes	planes	sixes	whales

One-Syllable Plural Nouns (-s)   **Two-Syllable Plural Nouns (-es)**

1. _____planes_____   11. _____

2. _____   12. _____

3. _____   13. _____

4. _____   14. _____

5. _____   15. _____

6. _____   16. _____

7. _____   17. _____

8. _____   18. _____

9. _____   19. _____

10. _____   20. _____

Count 1 point for each   _____ My Score
correctly sorted word.   20 Top Score

Word Building

 **Conventions Strategy**

Add -s, -es, or change f or fe to v and add -es to each singular noun below to make it plural.

Singular Nouns

1. puzzle _____puzzles_____
2. alley _____
3. leash _____
4. wife _____
5. desert _____

Plural Nouns

6. birch _____
7. joke _____
8. shelf _____
9. wrench _____
10. virus _____

Completing Sentences

Learning spelling patterns to make words plural helps you become a better speller and a better proofreader.

Conventions Strategy **Complete each sentence with the correct plural form of the singular noun in parentheses. Write the correct plural spelling on the line.**

1. Fewer than 500 Siberian (tiger) live on Earth.   ____tigers____
2. Snow (leopard) live in the mountains of central Asia.   _____
3. Wild (wolf) are living again in Yellowstone National Park. _____
4. Black uakari (monkey) live in Brazil.   _____
5. Australia's sleepy (lizard) can live as long as 30 years.   _____

Count 1 point for each correctly spelled word.   _____ My Score   15 Top Score

Adding -er, -est, -ed, and -ing

A **base word** is a word with no added parts. For base words ending in silent e, drop the e before adding the endings **-er**, **-est**, **-ed**, and **-ing**.

HINTS	EXAMPLES
The endings **-er** and **-est** are added to words to show comparisons.	white, whit<u>er</u>, whit<u>est</u>
Drop the silent e before adding **-er** or **-est** to words.	brave + er = braver brave + est = bravest
The ending **-ed** is added to most words to show an action that happened in the **past.**	hike, hik<u>ed</u>
The ending **-ing** is added to a word to show an action that is happening in the **present.**	hike, hik<u>ing</u>
Drop the silent e before adding **-ed** or **-ing** to most words.	dive + ed = dived dive + ing = diving
The **-ed** can sound different, but it is spelled **-ed** to show past action of most words.	poked has the /t/ sound pasted has the /id/ sound
Exceptions	**Examples**
Some words do not use **-ed** to show past action.	make/made, take/took, tell/told

Pattern Sort

Circle the words with the -est ending.

(bluest)	diving	loosest	prized	safest
braver	finest	making	ripest	tamer

Short Sort

Sorting words with the same base word can help you spell
words with different ending patterns.

 **Family Strategy** — **Sort each word in the box by writing it next to its base word.**

cuter	nicest	rarest	wider	safest
widest	cutest	safer	nicer	rarer
naming	tuned	baked	skating	tuning
scored	baking	skated	named	scoring

Base Words	*-er* Endings	*-est* Endings
1. safe	safer	
2. wide		
3. cute		
4. nice		
5. rare		

	-ed Endings	*-ing* Endings
6. bake		
7. tune		
8. name		
9. skate		
10. score		

Count 1 point for each
correctly sorted word.

_____ My Score
20 Top Score

Word Building

Adding endings to words can help you learn how to spell the different forms of those words.

 Conventions Strategy **Add the endings -ed and -ing to spell words that tell about the past and the present.**

Base Words	Add -ed (Past)	Add -ing (Present)
1. poke	poked	_____
2. rope	_____	_____
3. flame	_____	_____
4. like	_____	_____
5. blame	_____	_____

More Word Building

 Conventions Strategy **Add -er and -est to each base word below.**

Base Words	Add -er	Add -est
1. safe	safer	_____
2. true	_____	_____
3. close	_____	_____
4. little	_____	_____
5. weak	_____	_____

Subtracting Endings

Noticing how endings are added to base words can help you learn to add endings to other base words.

 **Conventions Strategy** — **Look carefully at each word with an ending. Remove the ending and add silent e. Write the base word on the line.**

Words with Endings	Base Words	Words with Endings	Base Words
1. hiked	hike	11. looser	_____
2. truest	_____	12. poked	_____
3. pasted	_____	13. moved	_____
4. braver	_____	14. finest	_____
5. pleasing	_____	15. diving	_____
6. skating	_____	16. whiter	_____
7. closest	_____	17. hoped	_____
8. graded	_____	18. nicer	_____
9. proving	_____	19. liking	_____
10. tamest	_____	20. wiring	_____

Count 1 point for each correctly spelled base word. _____ My Score
20 Top Score

Lesson **12**   **PROBLEM SOLVING**

Changing y to i

Many words end with the letter **y.** When adding the endings -es,
-er, and -est to some words that end in y, **change the y to i**
before adding the ending.

HINTS	EXAMPLES
Notice the letter **before** the **y** in a word.	ci<u>t</u>y, pen<u>n</u>y, si<u>ll</u>y, k<u>e</u>y
Change the y to i and add -es to make the plural form of nouns that end in *consonant-y*.	ba<u>by</u> + es = babies ci<u>ty</u> + es = cities
When adding -er or -est to a word that ends in *consonant-y*, change the y to i and add the ending.	sun<u>ny</u> + er = sunnier sun<u>ny</u> + est = sunniest
Remember that the endings -er and -est show comparisons.	crazy, crazier, craziest
When a noun ends in *vowel-y*, just add -s to make it plural.	b<u>oy</u> + s = boys k<u>ey</u> + s = keys

Pattern Sort

 Conventions Strategy

Write each word in the box beside the original form of the word ending in y.

bunnies	countries	funnier	pennies	silliest

1. bunny ___bunnies___   4. silly _____

2. funny _____   5. country _____

3. penny _____

Word Building

Learning to make nouns that end with a *consonant-y* plural will help you learn how to spell other words with the same spelling pattern.

 **Conventions Strategy** **Write the plural form of each noun ending with y. Notice the letter before the y.**

Nouns	Plurals	Nouns	Plurals
1. trophy	trophies	6. body	_____
2. pastry	_____	7. army	_____
3. turkey	_____	8. city	_____
4. treaty	_____	9. sky	_____
5. lady	_____	10. valley	_____

More Building

Noticing the *consonant-y* pattern can help you learn how to change the y to i when adding -er or -est to words.

 **Conventions Strategy** **Write the comparative forms of the words under the correct headings.**

	-er Ending	*-est* Ending
1. dingy	dingier	dingiest
2. weary	_____	_____
3. puny	_____	_____
4. early	_____	_____
5. dizzy	_____	_____

Count 1 point for each correctly spelled word in both exercises.

_____ My Score

20 Top Score

Look for Spelling Patterns

Thinking about how a word looks can help you spell the word.

 **Visualization Strategy**

Look carefully at the two spellings for each word. Circle the correct spelling of the word. Write the correct spelling on the line.

1. sillyer	(sillier)	sillier
2. stickier	skickyer	_____
3. bullies	bullyies	_____
4. juryes	juries	_____
5. wealthier	wealthyer	_____
6. cities	cityes	_____
7. injuryes	injuries	_____
8. windiest	windyest	_____
9. speedier	speedyer	_____
10. batteries	batteryes	_____
11. centurys	centuries	_____
12. cloudiest	cloudyest	_____
13. colonyes	colonies	_____
14. worries	worryes	_____
15. yummiest	yummyest	_____

Subtracting Endings and Suffixes

Taking away endings from words can help you notice how endings are added to words.

 **Conventions Strategy**

Look carefully at each word with an ending. Remove the ending and change the *i* back into a *y*. Write the base word on the line.

1. tackiest (− est) _____tacky_____

2. dairies (− es) _____

3. enemies (− es) _____

4. icier (− er) _____

5. factories (− es) _____

6. galleries (− es) _____

7. choppier (− er) _____

8. groceries (− es) _____

9. victories (− es) _____

10. tinier (− er) _____

11. laundries (− es) _____

12. ugliest (− est) _____

13. leafiest (− est) _____

14. greasier (− er) _____

15. luxuries (− es) _____

Count 1 point for each correctly spelled word.

_____ My Score
15 Top Score

Review Structural Patterns

These exercises review what you have learned in Lessons 10–12. Refer to those lessons if you have difficulty completing an exercise.

Lesson 10 Adding -s and -es

 **Look carefully at each singular noun. Write the plural form of the noun.**

Singular Nouns	Plural Nouns	Singular Nouns	Plural Nouns
1. ache	_____	6. diploma	_____
2. mess	_____	7. grass	_____
3. bargain	_____	8. headache	_____
4. shelf	_____	9. jewel	_____
5. clutch	_____	10. fox	_____

Lesson 11 Adding -er, -est, -ed, and -ing

 **Write the two words with endings next to the base word ending in silent e.**

Base Words	-ed Endings	-ing Endings
1. smile	_____	_____
2. tackle	_____	_____
3. locate	_____	_____

Base Words	-er Endings	-est Endings
4. cute	_____	_____
5. white	_____	_____

Count 1 point for each correctly spelled word in both exercises.   _____ My Score
20 Top Score

Name _____

Lesson 12 *Changing y to i*

Look at each pair of plural nouns carefully. Circle the correct spelling of the plural noun. Write the correct spelling on the line.

Plural Nouns

1. candy   candies   candyes   _____
2. jelly   jellyes   jellies   _____
3. hobby   hobbyes   hobbies   _____
4. monkey   monkeys   monkeies   _____
5. poppy   poppies   poppyes   _____

Cumulative Review

Read the following sentences. Cross out the ten misspelled words. Write the correct spelling above each misspelled word.

foggiest

One of the ~~foggyest~~ parts of America es at the mowth of the Columbia River in

Washington. It's gloomyer there thayn almost any other plase. More than 100

dayes with fog occur each yeer. Most familys would not chuse to live in such a

dreary area.

Count 1 point for each correctly spelled word. _____ My Score

15 Top Score

Lesson 13   **PROBLEM SOLVING**

Word Families: The Suffix -ion

A **suffix** is a letter or group of letters added to the end of a base word. When a suffix is added, the new word is part of the same **word family** as its base word. A suffix changes the meaning of the base word.

(base word) + (suffix) = (new word with new meaning)
construct   + **ion**   = construction

The suffix **-ion** has two meanings: "the action or process of" or "the result of."
completion, the action or process of completing
invention, the result of inventing

HINTS	EXAMPLES
For most base words, just add the suffix **-ion.**	abstract + **ion** = abstraction
When a base word ends in silent e, drop the e before adding **-ion.**	create − e + **ion** = creation
The way you say a base word is changed by the **-ion.**	Elect ends with the /t/ sound, but the /t/ sound changes to the /sh/ sound in election.
The suffix **-ion** makes the /ən/ sound. If you hear the /ən/ sound at the end of a word with a suffix, you know to spell the word with **-ion.**	emotion
Exceptions	**Examples**
Some base words that end in d, t, or silent e change their sound and spelling when -ion is added.	suspend + ion = suspension omit + ion = omission describe + ion = description

Change the Meaning

Adding the suffix *-ion* to a word can help you learn to spell new words with new meanings.

 **Conventions Strategy** **Drop the silent e and add the suffix *-ion* to each word to change its meaning.**

Base Words	Add *-ion*	Base Words	Add *-ion*
1. estimate	estimation	6. repress	
2. convict		7. digest	
3. project		8. decorate	
4. possess		9. televise	
5. subtract		10. intersect	

Think About the Meaning

Choosing words that make sense in text can help you learn the meanings of words with the *-ion* suffix.

 **Meaning Strategy** **Look at each pair of words in parentheses. Choose the word that makes the most sense in the sentence. Write the word on the line.**

1. You ____impress____ people by how you speak. (impress, impression)

2. You want to make a good _____. (impress, impression)

3. Car emissions _____ the air. (pollute, pollution)

4. _____ causes many people to become ill. (Pollute, Pollution)

5. Some parents _____ their children at home. (educate, education)

Count 1 point for each correctly spelled word _____ My Score
in the first exercise. Count 1 point for each
correctly chosen word in the second exercise.   15 Top Score

Change the Meaning

Taking away the suffix *-ion* from words can help you learn to spell base words.

 **Conventions Strategy** | **Take out the suffix *-ion* in each word and write the base word on the line.**

1. dedication _____dedicate_____

2. direction _____

3. prediction _____

4. attraction _____

5. devotion _____

6. confession _____

7. recession _____

8. suppression _____

9. fusion _____

10. revision _____

Knowing the Meaning

Knowing the meaning of the *-ion* suffix and base words can help you learn the meanings of many new words.

 **Meaning Strategy** | **Choose a word from the box that matches the definition. Write the word next to its meaning.**

| frustration | illustration | irrigation | perfection | revision |

1. the result of illustrating _____illustration_____

2. the result of being frustrated _____

3. the process of irrigating _____

4. the result of revising _____

5. the result of being perfect _____

Count 1 point for each correctly spelled word in the first exercise. Count 1 point for each correctly chosen word in the second exercise.

_____ My Score
15 Top Score   Word Families: The Suffix *-ion* • **59**

Think About the Meaning

Knowing the spellings and meanings of words with suffixes can
help you become a better speller and writer.

 **Meaning Strategy** | **Look at the words in parentheses. Choose the word in each pair that makes sense in the sentence. Write the correct word in the blank.**

1. (predict, prediction)   A poll is used to _____predict_____ how people will

   vote, but sometimes the _____ is wrong.

2. (direct, direction)   Police _____ traffic to get cars to go in

   the same _____.

3. (invent, invention)   Many people tried to _____ a flying

   machine, which one day resulted in the

   _____ of the airplane.

4. (extinct, extinction)   Dinosaurs are _____, but scientists do

   not agree on what caused their _____.

5. (supervise, supervision) If a teacher knows how to _____ the

   class, the students will have good _____.

6. (televise, television)   The networks will _____ a baseball

   game, so everyone can see it on _____.

7. (illustrate, illustration)   The _____ on a book's cover is drawn

   by an artist who knows how to _____.

8. (irrigate, irrigation)   Farmers _____ their fields.

Count 1 point for each
correctly chosen word.

_____ My Score
15 Top Score

Word Families: The Suffixes -*ness* and -*en*

Remember, a **suffix** is a letter or group of letters added to the end of a base word. The suffix -**ness** means "state, quality, condition, or degree."

bright + ness = brightness

The suffix -**en** means "to cause to be," "to cause to have," or "made of, resemble."

gold + en = golden

HINTS	EXAMPLES
Adding the suffix -**ness** does not change the spelling of most base words.	brave, braveness
If a base word ends in y, change y to *i* before adding -**ness.**	silly + ness = silliness
If a base word ends in silent e, drop the e before adding -**en.**	ripe + en = ripen
Adding -**ness** or -**en** to a base word adds another syllable.	*gold* has one syllable *golden* has two syllables
When you add the suffix -**en** to a *short vowel + consonant* word like *mad,* double the consonant.	red + en = redden sad + en = sadden

Sort by Suffixes

 Family Strategy

Circle the -*ness* or -*en* suffix in the words below.

cheapen	darkness	harden	politeness	tenderness

Count 2 points for each correctly circled suffix.

_____ My Score

10 Top Score

Lesson 14

Sort It Out

Sorting words in the same family can help you spell words with suffixes.

 **Family Strategy** **Write each word in the box beside the word in the same family.**

awareness	dizziness	quietness	taken	ugliness
cheeriness	promptness	sharpen	truthfulness	wooden

1. ugly   _____ugliness_____
2. quiet   _____
3. aware   _____
4. take   _____
5. cheery   _____

6. prompt   _____
7. sharp   _____
8. wood   _____
9. dizzy   _____
10. truthful   _____

Meaning Match

Learning the meanings of suffixes can help you learn the meanings of new words.

 **Meaning Strategy** **Write the words from the box beside their meanings.**

blueness	boldness	golden	soften	thicken

1. state of being bold   _____boldness_____
2. degree of blue   _____
3. made of gold   _____

4. becomes soft   _____
5. causes to be thick   _____

Count 1 point for each correctly chosen word in both exercises.

_____ My Score
15 Top Score

Word Building

Learning the rules for adding suffixes to base words can help
you spell words in the same word family.

 **Family Strategy** **Write the two words with suffixes on the lines beside the base word.**

Base Words	Add -*en*	Add -*ness*
1. hard	harden	hardness
2. tough		
3. soft		
4. broad		
5. white		
6. stiff		
7. sharp		
8. quick		
9. ripe		
10. sick		
11. moist		
12. bright		
13. loose		
14. flat		
15. sad		

Count 1 point
for each correctly
spelled word.   _____ My Score
                       30 Top Score   **Word Families: The Suffixes** -*ness* **and** -*en* • **63**

Word Choices

 **Meaning Strategy** | **Read each sentence carefully. Think about the meanings of the two words in parentheses. Write the word that makes sense in the blank.**

1. (fond, fondness)   The two hikers had a ____fondness____ for hiking.

2. (peaceful, peacefulness) They always enjoyed the _____ of it.

3. (cold, coldness)   The _____ air made their breath frosty.

4. (red, redden)   Their faces began to _____ from the cold.

5. (bright, brightness)   The _____ of the snow blinded them.

Word Building

Adding -ness to words with other suffixes can help you learn to spell more words.

 **Family Strategy** | **Add the suffix -ness to make another word in the same family.**

Base Words	Base Words with One Suffix	Add the Suffix -ness
1. sense	sensitive	____sensitiveness____
2. attract	attractive	_____
3. care	careful	_____
4. help	helpful	_____
5. clean	cleanly	_____

Count 1 point for each correctly chosen word in the first exercise. Count 1 point for each correctly spelled word in the second exercise.

_____ My Score
10 Top Score

Lesson 15 PROBLEM SOLVING

Silent Letters (g, gn, kn, mb, wr)

Most consonant letters spell their consonant sounds. Some words are spelled with **silent consonant letters.** Silent letters are usually part of consonant blends.

The letter **g** is silent in the blend **gn** at the beginning or end of a word.

gnome, sign

The letter **k** is silent in the blend **kn** at the beginning of a word.

knight

The letter **b** is silent in the blend **mb** at the end of a word.

thumb

The letter **w** is silent in the blend **wr** at the beginning of a word.

write

HINTS
The blend **kn** is never used at the end of a word.
The blend **mb** is never used at the beginning of a word.
The blend **wr** is never used at the end of a word.

Exceptions	Examples
The **g** is not silent in a word in which **gn** is divided into syllables.	sig-nal, dig-ni-ty
Some words have **mb** followed by **le.** In these words the **b** is not silent.	thimble, tumble, crumble

Silent Sort

Say each word. Circle the silent letters in the words.

gnome	design	knife	tomb	written

Count 2 points for each correctly circled letter.

_____ My Score
10 Top Score

Silent Letters • **65**

Lesson 15

EXAMINE

Sound Sort

Sorting words by their sounds can help you spell words with the same sounds.

 **Pronunciation Strategy**

Say and sort each word in the box under the sound heard in the blend.

| knot | know | jamb | gnaw | gnarl |
| wreck | gnat | knife | tomb | wrap |

/n/

1. _____gnat_____   4. _____

2. _____   5. _____

3. _____   6. _____

/m/

7. _____

8. _____

/r/

9. _____

10. _____

Visualization Strategy

Sort the words in the box below their consonant blends.

| knoll | lamb | wrong | resign | assign |
| knuckle | dumb | knock | wreath | align |

gn

1. _____align_____   4. _____

2. _____   5. _____

3. _____   6. _____

kn

4. _____

5. _____

6. _____

mb

7. _____

8. _____

wr

9. _____

10. _____

Count 1 point for each correctly sorted word in both exercises.

_____ My Score
20 Top Score

Name _____

Lesson 15   EXTEND

Points for Proofreading

Proofreading can help you learn how to find misspelled words.

 **Visualization Strategy**

Look at each pair of words carefully. Circle the word with the correct spelling. Write the correct spelling on the line.

1. bom   (bomb)   ___bomb___
2. wrong   rong   _____
3. naw   gnaw   _____
4. num   numb   _____
5. wrist   rist   _____

6. clim   climb   _____
7. nead   knead   _____
8. knife   nife   _____
9. nu   gnu   _____
10. lamb   lam   _____

Blend Choices

Thinking about how a word looks can help you spell the word.

 **Visualization Strategy**

Add the missing consonant blends: _gn_, _kn_, _mb_, or _wr_ in the blanks to spell real words. Write the real words on the lines.

1. desi __gn__   ___design___
2. la _____   _____
3. si _____   _____
4. _____ ote   _____
5. cli _____   _____

6. _____ ob   _____
7. _____ ench   _____
8. to _____   _____
9. _____ ome   _____
10. _____ eath   _____

Count 1 point for each correctly spelled word.

_____ My Score
20 Top Score

Silent Letters • **67**

Name _____

Dictionary Dig

Looking in a dictionary can help you learn how to correctly spell and say words.

Dictionary Strategy

Look up each word in the dictionary to find out whether the g in the word is silent. Rewrite each word on the line. Circle "silent" if the g is a silent letter.

1. dignity _____dignity_____ silent

2. assignment _____ silent

3. resignation _____ silent

4. alignment _____ silent

5. designer _____ silent

6. malignant _____ silent

7. cologne _____ silent

8. gnarled _____ silent

9. consignment _____ silent

10. signify _____ silent

11. gnash _____ silent

12. designate _____ silent

13. gneiss _____ silent

14. sign _____ silent

15. gnu _____ silent

Count 1 point for each correctly spelled word. Count 1 point for each correctly circled answer.

_____ My Score

25 Top Score

Name _____

Review Meaning Patterns

These exercises review what you have learned in Lessons 13–15.
Refer to those lessons if you have difficulty completing an exercise.

Lesson 13 Word Families: The Suffix -ion

 **Add -ion to each base word to make a new word.**

Base Words	New Words	Base Words	New Words
1. impress	_____	6. rotate	_____
2. calculate	_____	7. confess	_____
3. donate	_____	8. locate	_____
4. operate	_____	9. revise	_____
5. elect	_____	10. attract	_____

Lesson 14 Word Families: The Suffixes -ness and -en

 **Add -ness to the first list of words. Add -en to the second list of words.**

Add -ness		Add -en	
1. ugly	_____	6. moist	_____
2. tough	_____	7. sharp	_____
3. thankful	_____	8. cheap	_____
4. bold	_____	9. red	_____
5. polite	_____	10. length	_____

Count 1 point for each   _____ My Score
correctly spelled word in   20 Top Score
both exercises.

Name _____

Lesson 15 *Silent Letters*

 **Visualization Strategy**

Look carefully at each pair of words. Circle the word with the correct spelling. Write the correct spelling on the line.

1. align   alin   _____
2. nock   knock   _____
3. gnarl   narl   _____
4. wriggle   riggle   _____
5. nuckle   knuckle   _____
6. nu   gnu   _____
7. comb   com   _____
8. wreck   reck   _____
9. noll   knoll   _____
10. crum   crumb   _____

11. gnat   nat   _____
12. nob   knob   _____
13. rench   wrench   _____
14. lamb   lam   _____
15. tomb   tom   _____
16. ritten   written   _____
17. desin   design   _____
18. malign   malin   _____
19. restle   wrestle   _____
20. cologne   colone   _____

Cumulative Review

 **Proofreading Strategy**

Read the following sentences. Cross out the ten misspelled words. Write the correct spelling above each misspelled word.

There ~~es~~ is much confuzun about the gnu. Many people do not noe anything about

this animle. The gnu is a larj antelope that lifes in Africa. It eets twigs, leaves, and

gras. The nu is sometimes kalled a wildebeest.

Count 1 point for each correctly spelled word in both exercises.   _____ My Score
30 Top Score

70   UNIT 5 Review: *Meaning Patterns*

Homophones

Homophones are words that sound the same as one another, but have different spellings and different meanings.

HINTS	EXAMPLES
Homophones can have different spellings for the same vowel sounds.	_Rode_ sounds like _road_.
Homophones can have different spellings for the same consonant sounds.	_Guessed_ sounds like _guest_.
Homophones can have silent letters.	_Knew_ sounds like _gnu_ and _new_.
Homophones can be made with contractions.	_I'll_ sounds like _aisle_.
Exceptions	**Example**
Homophones can have two words.	_I scream_ sounds like _ice cream_.

Homophone Sort

Pronunciation Strategy

Sort each word in the box by writing it beside the homophone with the same sound.

| piece | four | buy | whole | sale |

1. by ___buy___
2. sail _____
3. peace _____
4. for _____
5. hole _____

Sort Homophones by Meanings

Sorting words by homophone clues can help you learn the
spellings and the meanings of the homophones.

 **Meaning Strategy**   **Read each phrase carefully. Each underlined word
is a homophone of one of the words in the box.
Match each word in the box to its homophone clue.
Write the correct spelling on the line.**

cheep	knows	peace	sale	sun
heard	mane	peel	scent	through

1. a <u>herd</u> of elephants   _____heard_____ the noise

2. the <u>main</u> thing   a horse's _____

3. a <u>piece</u> of pie   _____ for all people

4. a <u>son</u> and his father   the bright _____

5. <u>threw</u> the ball   flew _____ the sky

6. a red <u>nose</u>   _____ spelling

7. <u>sent</u> the letter   the _____ of a rose

8. a <u>cheap</u> toy   a baby bird's _____

9. the boat's <u>sail</u>   buy on _____

10. the <u>peal</u> of the bell   _____ the potatoes

Count 1 point for each
correctly chosen word.   _____ My Score
                                10 Top Score

Lesson 16 EXTEND

Homophone Choices

| Meaning Strategy | **Look carefully at each pair of homophones. Write the homophone that makes sense in each blank.** |

hoarse, horse

1. A cowboy can become _____hoarse_____ from calling his
_____horse_____.

ewe, you

2. Did _____ know that a _____ is
a female sheep?

tail, tale

3. This is a funny _____ about a dog's
_____.

for, four

4. You can paint _____ pictures
_____ your mother.

heard, herd

5. I _____ that a _____ of cattle
can be very loud.

pail, pale

6. We filled a _____ with _____
yellow paint for the kitchen walls.

wood, would

7. A lumberjack _____ chop _____.

night, knight

8. A _____ stays in his castle at
_____.

nose, knows

9. A doctor _____ how to set a broken
_____.

threw, through

10. When he _____ the ball, it went
_____ the window.

Count 1 point for each
correctly chosen word.

_____ My Score
20 Top Score

Homophones • 73

Lesson **16**

STRETCH

Homophone Choices

Seeing homophones together can help you learn to choose the correct words within a sentence.

 **Meaning Strategy**

Carefully read each pair of homophones. Write the homophone that makes sense in the sentence. Check the dictionary for the homophone meanings you do not know.

sighs, size   1. What ____size____ is your shoe?

wears, wares   2. A safe person _____ a helmet when riding a bike.

berry, bury   3. A dog will _____ a bone in the yard.

throne, thrown   4. A queen sits on a _____.

maze, maize   5. Another word for corn is _____.

dear, deer   6. Many _____ are in the forest.

beat, beet   7. Sports teams try to _____ each other in competitions.

fowl, foul   8. A _____ is a penalty in basketball.

ate, eight   9. Some schools begin at _____ o'clock.

some, sum   10. The _____ of 78 + 95 is 173.

hair, hare   11. Another name for a rabbit is a _____.

grown, groan   12. A _____ boy is called a man.

tense, tents   13. Scout troops often sleep in _____.

rap, wrap   14. Please _____ this birthday present for me.

urn, earn   15. You can _____ money by mowing people's grass.

Count 1 point for each correctly chosen word.   _____ My Score

15 Top Score

Contractions

A **contraction** is a word formed from two or more words. When the words come together, some letters are taken out, and an apostrophe (') marks the place.

HINTS	EXAMPLES
Only one letter is taken out of some contractions.	I am − a = I'm
Many letters are taken out of some contractions.	I would − woul = I'd they have − ha = they've
The first word in the pair that makes a contraction usually keeps all of its letters.	have not = <u>have</u>n't
Entire words are left out of some contractions.	of the clock = o'clock
Some contractions are homophones.	I'll/aisle; he'll/heal
Make sure you put the apostrophe (') in the right place.	*haven't* (not *have'nt*)
Leaving out the apostrophe can spell a different word.	*I'll* becomes the word *ill*
Only one contraction is made with the word *am*.	I'm
Only one contraction is made with the word *us*.	let's
Some contractions look the same, but mean two different things.	*he'd* means *he would* and *he had* *she's* means *she has* and *she is*
Exception	**Example**
One contraction changes the spelling and the sound of the omitted letters.	*will not* becomes *won't* (not *willn't*)

Sort It Out

Sorting contractions by their word meaning patterns can help
you spell contractions.

 **Meaning Strategy**

**Sort the contractions in the boxes under their word
meaning patterns.**

| haven't | he's | isn't | it'll | she'll |

not

1. ____isn't____

2. _____

will

3. _____

4. _____

is

5. _____

| he'd | I've | they'd | they're | you've |

have

1. _____

2. _____

had

3. _____

4. _____

are

5. _____

| I'm | let's | there'd | we'd | where's |

would

1. _____

2. _____

is

3. _____

am

4. _____

us

5. _____

Count 1 point for each
correctly sorted word.

_____ My Score

15 Top Score

Word Building

Thinking about how a word looks can help you spell the word.

Conventions Strategy

Build a contraction from the two words. Think about how the contraction should look and where the apostrophe should go. Spell the contraction on the line.

1. we   + have   _we've_

2. I   + will   _____

3. do   + not   _____

4. they   + have   _____

5. here   + is   _____

6. should + not   _____

7. that   + will   _____

8. we   + are   _____

9. I   + am   _____

10. they   + will   _____

11. could + not   _____

12. they   + are   _____

13. has   + not   _____

14. she   + had   _____

15. she   + would   _____

Choosing Contractions

Thinking about what a word means can help you learn to spell the word.

 **Meaning Strategy**

Write a contraction from the box that is a homophone for each word.

he'll	rain's	we'd	we'll	we've

1. wheel _____we'll_____

2. weave _____

3. heal _____

4. weed _____

5. reigns _____

Adding an Apostrophe

Thinking about what a word means can help you spell the word.

 **Conventions Strategy**

Keeping the same letters, add an apostrophe in the correct place to make each word a contraction. Write the contraction on the line.

1. shed _____she'd_____

2. shell _____

3. were _____

4. well _____

5. wed _____

Count 1 point for each correctly spelled contraction.

_____ My Score
10 Top Score

Lesson 18   **PROBLEM SOLVING**

Greek Spelling Patterns (*ph* for /f/)

Many words spell the /f/ sound with the letters *ph*, as in *phone*.
The *ph* spelling is found in many words with **Greek roots.**
Greek roots are word parts from the Greek language. Roots
have certain meanings and combine with other words.

Greek Roots	Meanings	Examples
graph	to write	*autograph*
phon, phone	sound	*telephone*
photo	light	*photograph*
phys	nature	*physical*

HINTS	EXAMPLES
When you hear the /f/ sound in an unfamiliar word with a Greek root, spell it with a *ph*.	/f/ as in *photocell*
Words with the same Greek root are in the same word family.	*physical/physician*
Some words are made up of two Greek roots.	*photo* + *graph* = *photograph*
Some words used today are shortened forms of Greek roots.	*telephone/phone*, *photograph/photo*

Short Sort

Pronunciation
Strategy

**Circle the letters that make the /f/ sound in each
word.**

autogra**ph**	phone	photo	physical	telephone

Count 2 points for each
correctly circled word.   _____ My Score
                                10 Top Score   Greek Spelling Patterns • **79**

Lesson 18

Sort It Out

Sorting unfamiliar words by their root patterns will help you spell other words with the same roots.

 **Family Strategy** | **Sort the words in the boxes below their Greek roots.**

| biography | digraph | megaphone | paragraph | phonics |

graph (to write)

1. _____

2. _____

3. _____

phon, phone (sound)

4. _____

5. _____

| photocopier | physique | physiotherapy | photogenic | physician |

phys (nature)

1. _____

2. _____

3. _____

photo (light)

4. _____

5. _____

Count 1 point for each correctly sorted word.

_____ My Score
10 Top Score

The Right Look

Thinking about how a word looks can help you learn how to spell it.

 **Visualization Strategy**

Sort each word in the box under the word that has the same spelling for the /f/ sound.

knife	photographer	food	flute	physical
family	afternoon	frame	atmosphere	firefly
phonograph	Friday	half	geography	Phil
grandfather	elephant	phony	physician	headphone

/f/ spelled *ph*

1. _____elephant_____
2. _____
3. _____
4. _____
5. _____
6. _____
7. _____
8. _____
9. _____
10. _____

/f/ spelled *f*

11. _____
12. _____
13. _____
14. _____
15. _____
16. _____
17. _____
18. _____
19. _____
20. _____

Count 1 point for each correctly sorted word. _____ My Score
20 Top Score

Greek Spelling Patterns • **81**

Meaningful Roots

Knowing the meanings of Greek roots can help you begin to understand the meanings of many challenging words.

 **Meaning Strategy**

Look for the Greek root in each challenging word in the box. Think about the meanings of the different Greek roots. Write each word from the box under the meaning of the Greek root found in the word.

calligraphy	bibliography	physicist	phonogram	telephoto
telegraph	choreography	polyphonic	autograph	photometry
geophysics	photosynthesis	microphone	saxophone	cacophony

to write

1. _____calligraphy_____

2. _____

3. _____

4. _____

5. _____

nature

6. _____

7. _____

sound

8. _____

9. _____

10. _____

11. _____

12. _____

light

13. _____

14. _____

15. _____

Count 1 point for each correctly sorted word.

_____ My Score
15 Top Score

Name _____

Review Meaning Patterns

These exercises review what you have learned in Lessons
16–18. Refer to those lessons if you have difficulty completing
an exercise.

Lesson 16 Homophones

 **Look carefully at each pair of homophones. Write the homophones in the blanks where they make sense in each sentence.**

or, ore   **1.** Iron _____ is used for making metal.

sent, scent   **2.** Long ago, women _____ letters on stationary

                      with a pleasant _____.

tide, tied   **3.** A tightly _____ lure on the end of a fishing line

                      will be fine in a strong _____.

Lesson 17 Contractions

 **Write the contraction made from the two words on the line.**

1. was + not   _____

2. they + had   _____

3. we + are   _____

4. let + us   _____

5. she + will   _____

Count 1 point for each correctly chosen word.   _____ My Score
Count 1 point for each correctly spelled contraction.   10 Top Score

Name _____

Lesson 18 Greek Roots (/f/ spelled *ph*)

 Meaning Strategy **Sort each word in the box by writing it under the Greek root for that word.**

| telegraph | photographer | physical | telephone | telephoto |
| phonics | physician | geography | photogenic | physique |

photo   **phys**   **phon, phone**   **graph**

1. _____   4. _____   7. _____   9. _____

2. _____   5. _____   8. _____   10. _____

3. _____   6. _____

Cumulative Review

 Proofreading Strategy **Read the following sentences. Cross out the ten misspelled words. Write the correct spelling above each misspelled word.**

                      man

In 1876, an American ~~mann~~ invented the ferst commercial telefone. His naim was

Alexander Graham Bell. By the yeer 1915, people could make phon kalls to

different states. They were so happy that they di'dnt have to travel to talc to their

friends and familys.

Count 1 point for each correctly sorted word in the first exercise.   _____ My Score
Count 1 point for each correctly spelled word in the second exercise.   20 Top Score

Sound Spellings

1. _____   ape

2. _____   home

3. _____   huge

4. _____   feet

5. _____   flat

6. _____   drum

7. _____   wild

8. _____   feed

9. _____   sit

10. _____   shy

Count 1 point for each correctly spelled word.

_____ My Score
10 Top Score

Name _____

Sound Spelling Patterns

1. _____   mouse

2. _____   fur

3. _____   round

4. _____   front

5. _____   hear

6. _____   dark

7. _____   stand

8. _____   destroy

9. _____   fear

10. _____   enjoy

Count 1 point for each correctly spelled word.

_____ My Score
10 Top Score

Name _____

Sound Spelling Patterns

1. _____   share

2. _____   myth

3. _____   teach

4. _____   slave

5. _____   forest

6. _____   queens

7. _____   gold

8. _____   huge

9. _____   swan

10. _____   stuck

Count 1 point for   _____ My Score
each correctly   10 Top Score
spelled word.

Structural Patterns

1. _____ | insects

2. _____ | butterflies

3. _____ | roaches

4. _____ | living

5. _____ | coldest

6. _____ | lived

7. _____ | largest

8. _____ | tiniest

9. _____ | heavier

10. _____ | bodies

Count 1 point for each correctly spelled word.

_____ My Score
10 Top Score

Meaning Patterns

1. _____   sign

2. _____   digestion

3. _____   wrong

4. _____   ripen

5. _____   tasteless

6. _____   known

7. _____   knife

8. _____   golden

9. _____   invention

10. _____   connection

Count 1 point for each correctly spelled word.

_____ My Score

10 Top Score

Meaning Patterns

1. _____ | telegraph

2. _____ | heard

3. _____ | doesn't

4. _____ | that's

5. _____ | telephone

6. _____ | can't

7. _____ | would

8. _____ | photography

9. _____ | whole

10. _____ | let's

Count 1 point for
each correctly
spelled word.

_____ My Score
10 Top Score

Easily Misspelled Words

Why Do We Misspell Words?

Spelling can be easy if you know the spelling patterns. The words below are hard to spell because they do not follow regular patterns. These words can be confused with other words that have the same sound. For words that do not follow spelling patterns, you must memorize the spellings and make up your own spelling clues.

accept	its
again	it's
almost	jewel
always	movie
animal	ninth
answer	nothing
are	once
babies	other
because	people
charge	principal
children	quiet
choir	said
color	sandwich
dear	special
deer	their
double	trouble
doubt	were
eighth	we're
friend	your
guess	you're

Help for Spelling Easily Misspelled Words

First, ask yourself these questions:

1. Is the word a **HOMOPHONE**? their (there)

2. Are there **SILENT LETTERS** in the word? were (silent e)
   guess (silent u)

3. Is the word an **IRREGULAR PLURAL?** people (person)

4. Does the **VOWEL SOUND** not sound like its spelling? friend double
   people movie

5. Is the **VOWEL SOUND** in a long vowel pattern with a short sound? said (/e/)

Second, think of strategies that will help you memorize the correct spellings:

1. Think of **RHYMING WORDS** that have the same spelling. double (trouble)
   other (mother)

2. Find words that are in the same **FAMILY** as the word. again   (gain)
   always   (way)
   almost   (most)

3. Think of how the word should **LOOK.** friend (not frend)
   once (not wonce)

4. Make up your own ways of memorizing the spellings. You gain if you try
   it again.